MOSAICS AND CERAMIC ARTS [USES IN BANGLADESH]

Bangladesh covers 143, 998sq.km area in between the Himalayan ranges and the Bay of Bengal for which the G.P.S. is Lat. 26°41' N. and long. 92°41' to 88°02'E. The major part of this vast terrain is formed of river-borne new alluvial deposits which is flat in contour while the rest represents smaller sporadic belts formed of older alluvium with a little elevation above the general height of the country. However, at different corners of its length a vast number of archaeological sites and monuments, mostly belonging to the medieval period, are lying at random.

In art history, ceramics and ceramic art mean art objects such as figures, tiles, and tableware made from clay and other raw materials by the process of pottery. Some ceramicproducts are regarded as fine art, while others are regarded as decorative, industrial orapplied art objects, or as artifacts in archaeology. They may be made by one individual or in a factory where a group of people design, make and decorate the ware. Decorative ceramics are sometimes called "art pottery".[1]

The word "ceramics" comes from the Greek keramikos (κεραμικος), meaning "pottery", which in turn comes from keramos (κεραμος), meaning "potter's clay."[2] Most traditional ceramic products were made from clay (or clay mixed with other materials), shaped and subjected to heat, and tableware and decorative ceramics are generally still made this way. In modern ceramic engineering usage, ceramics is the art and science of making objects from inorganic, non-metallic

materials by the action of heat. It
excludes glass and mosaicmade from glass tesserae.

There is a long history of ceramic art in almost all developed cultures, and often ceramic objects are all the artistic evidence left from vanished cultures, like that of the Nok in Africa over 2,000 years ago. Cultures especially noted for ceramics include the Chinese, Cretan,Greek, Persian, Mayan, Japanese, and Korean cultures, as well as the modern Western cultures.

Elements of ceramic art, upon which different degrees of emphasis have been placed at different times, are the shape of the object, its decoration by painting, carving and other methods, and the glazing found on most ceramics.

Ceramics and ceramic is the art of creating images with an assemblage of small pieces of colored glass, stone, or other materials. It is a technique of **decorative** or interior decoration. Most mosaics are made of small, flat, roughly square, pieces of stone or glass of different colors, known as tesserae; but mosaics, especially floor mosaics, may also be made of small rounded pieces of stone, and called "pebble mosaics".

Ceramic Art : The ceramic and inlay decoration too were profusely used in the Mughal buildings. In the time of Akbar, the mosaics were made from small tesserae which were combined in Persian geometrical patterns. But in Jahangir's reign pietra-dura began to be utilized for inlay work. The earliest example of the use of pietra-dura inlay seems to have been made in celebrated Jag Mandir water-palace in the Pichola Lake at Udaipur and the Itmad-ud-daulah's tomb at Agra. In the time of Shah Jahan pietra-dura superseded the older mosaic ornamentation. Many of Shah Jahan's buildings in the forts of Delhi and Agra were decorated with pietra-dura inlay. Jahangir's tomb at Shandara, the Sheesh Mahal in Lahore and the Taj Mahal at Agra are fine examples of the beautiful ornamentation of the pietra-dura art.

Mughal Emperor Akbar encouraged the art of sculpture. He had the statues of Jai Mal and Fatha, the Rajput heroes of Chittor, seated on elephants, carved out of stone, and had them placed at the gate of the Agra Fort. The elephant gateway of Fatehpur sikri is still guarded by the mutilated figures of two colossal elephants, perched on supports 12.5 feet high, whose trunks were originally inter-locked across the entrance.

Mughal Emperor Jahangir too had two life-size marble statues of Rana Amar Singh and his son Karan Singh made and erected in the palace garden at Agra below the Jharokha-Darshan. We have no evidence to show that Shah Jahan encouraged the art of sculpture. It is a matter of common knowledge that Aurangzeb was positively against it and the art, therefore, started disappeared for want of patronage.

Decorative Carving : The Mughals were lovers of decorative relief carving and embellished their buildings with this art. The delicate marble carving on the walls of the uppermost terrace of Akbar's tomb at Sikandra is of 52 different varieties. Besides, the building is embellished with representations of clouds, plants, flowers, butterflies, insects, and a conventional vase design. Relief carving was supposed to be indispensable in high class Mughal buildings. Marble screen work carved in stone was equally fashionable. The marble work in the Taj Mahal, show that in the reign of Akbar and Shah Jahan the artist could produce masterpieces
Mughal culture and refinement are best reflected in stone. More than any other forms of art, architecture depends upon rich patrons.

As the might of the Mughal Empire spread and as the great Mughal emperors grew richer, more and more outstanding buildings were constructed in which Muslim motifs were to be found side by side with local Indian traditions.

4

Akbar's reign struck a new role in Indo-Muslim architecture. Among his buildings,palaces and fort complex at Fatehpur Sikri, the Jodha Bai Palace, Diwan-i-Am, Diwan-i-Khas, Jami Masjid, Panch Mahal and Buland Darwaja—are most impressive. Akbar took keen interest in the work of construction both at Agra and Fatehpur Sikri. In these buildings Persian and Central Asian influence are conspicuous in the glazed blue tiles used for decoration in the walls or for tiling the roofs. In the construction of Buland Darwaja the Iranian influence was conspicuous. Jahangir was not a prolific builder. But his one great work, the tomb of his father at Sikandra, is a highly interesting structure, constructed somewhat in the manner of a Buddhist Vihara.

Shah Jahan's reign marked the heyday of rich splendor in architecture. During Shah Jahan's reign fine white marble encrusted with semi-precious and sometimes even precious stones became the main decorative material used in architecture, especially in Delhi and Agra. The Diwan-i-Am, Diwan-i-Khas and Jami Masjid at Delhi and the Moti Masjid at Agra are among his stateliest constructions. But Shah Jahan is famous as the builder of Taj Mahal, that 'miracle of miracles' which is justly regarded as a jewel of the builder's art. He built it at Agra in the memory of his beloved wife Mumtaz Mahal.
The Mughal architectural traditions influenced the architecture of other parts of the country.

The Middle age of Bengal coincided with Muslim rule. Out of about 550 years of Muslim rule, Bengal was only ruled by Delhi-based All-India empires for almost 200 years. For approximately 350 years, Bengal remained virtually independent. The Muslim rule of Bengal is usually divided into three phases. The first phase, which lasted from 1204 to 1342, witnessed the consolidation of Muslim rule in Bengal. It was characterized by extreme political instability. The second phase, which spanned the period 1342 to 1575, saw the emergence of independent local dynasties such as the Ilyas Shahi dynasty (1342-1414), the dynasty of King Ganesha (1414-1442) and Husain Shahi dynasty (l493-1539). The third phase, which lasted from 1575 to 1757, witnessed the emergence of a centralized administration in Bengal within the framework of the Mughal empire. The Mughal viceroys in Bengal curbed the independence of powerful landlords who were known as Bara Bhuiyas and suppressed Portuguese pirates who frequently interfered with the flow of foreign trade.

Muslim rule in the region is marked by two major achievements. First, prior to Muslim rule in this area, Bengal was an ever-shifting mosaic of principalities. The natural limits of Bengal were not clearly perceived until its political unification by the Ilyas Shahi rulers in the 14th century. Secondly, the political unity fashioned by the Muslim rulers also promoted linguistic homogeneity. Unlike their predecessors, the Muslim rulers were ardent patrons of Bengali language and literature. Prior to Muslim rule, the Bengali vernacular was despised for its impurities and vulgarities by Hindu elites who were the beneficiaries and champions of Sanskrit education. The spread of Islam challenged the spiritual leadership of upper caste Hindus. The intense competition between Islam and resurgent Hinduism in the form of Vaisnavism for capturing the imagination of the unlettered masses resulted in an outpouring of their stirring messages in the vernacular Bengali language.

The Muslim rule of Bengal also witnessed the gradual expansion of Islam in this region. Contrary to popular beliefs, the Muslim rulers in Bengal were not in the least idealists or proselytizers; they were primarily adventurers whose sole aim was to perpetuate their own rule. The preponderance of Muslims in Bangladesh region stands out in striking contrast to the singular failure of Muslims in converting local people in other parts of northern and southern India. The distribution of Muslims in different regions of South Asia clearly contradicts the hypothesis that the patronage of the temporal authority was the most crucial variable in the spread of Islam. If this hypothesis was correct there would have been Muslim preponderance in areas around the seats of Muslim rule in northern India. The fact that the Muslims remained an insignificant minority in the Delhi region where they ruled for more than six hundred years clearly suggests that Islam in South Asia was not imposed from above. In Bengal, the share of Muslims in the total population was higher in areas remote from the seats of Muslim rule.

Islam was propagated in the Bangladesh region by a large number of Muslims who were mostly active from the 14th to 16th centuries. Among these missionaries, Hazrat Shah Jalal, Rasti Shah, Khan Jahan Ali, Shaikh Sharafuddin Abu Tawamah, Shah

Makhdoom Ruposh, Shaikh Baba Adam Shahid, Shah Sultan Mahisawar, Shaikh Alauddin Alaul Huq and Shah Ali Bagdadi deserve special mention. While similar Muslim missionary activities failed in other regions of South Asia, Islam ultimately succeeded in penetrating deeply into Bengal because the social environment of this region was congenial to the diffusion of a new religion. In much of South Asia, strong village communities were impenetrable barriers to the spread of alien faiths.

In Bengal, the corporateness of village institutions was weak in eastern areas; it gradually increased towards the western areas. The distribution of Muslim population also followed a similar spatial pattern in this region. The Muslims in Bengal were concentrated in the eastern areas and the share of Hindu population was much higher in western areas.

The Muslim rule of Bengal contributed to economic polarization and cultural dichotomy. Except the brief interludes of the northern Indian empires, pre-Muslim Bengal was ruled by local potentates. Most of the Muslim rulers either acted as agents of Delhi or tried to use Bengal as a stepping stone for attaining political authority in Delhi. Economic exploitation intensified during this period owing to transfer of resources to northern India. The main victims of this exploitative system were locally converted Muslims and low caste Hindus. The sole aim of the Muslim rulers was to mobilize as much resources as possible. The size of the immigrant Muslim ruling elite was small. Furthermore, different factions of the ruling elite did not trust each other. Consequently, Muslim rule in Bengal became a coalition of immigrant Muslims and upper caste Hindus.

The gradual process of conversion to Islam in Bengal resulted in an intense interaction between Islam and Hinduism. At the folk level, however, there was less confrontation and more interaction between Hinduism and Islam. A syncretic tradition developed around the cult and pantheons of pirs. The actual practices of local Muslim converts were an anathema to both Hindu and Muslim religious leaders. The orthodox Hindus, despite their political reconciliation with Muslim rulers, despised the local Muslims as untouchables (Mlechhas). The Muslim religious leaders were equally scornful of the customs and practices of local converts. Hated by immigrant religious leaders for their ways of life and by the local aristocracy for their adherence to an alien faith, local converts faced a dichotomy of faith and habitat which found expression in an emotional conflict between religion and language. This dichotomy can be traced in Bengali literature as early as the fourteenth century. 'Those who are born in Bengal but hate Bengali language", asserted the 17th century poet Abdul Hakim "had doubtful parentage. Those who are not satisfied with their mother tongue should migrate to other lands".

The earliest known examples of Ceramic/mosaics made of different materials were found at a temple building in Abra, Mesopotamia, and are dated to the second half of 3rd millennium BC. They consist of pieces of colored stones, shells and ivory. Excavations at Susa and Chogha Zanbil show evidence of the first glazed tiles, dating from around 1500 BC. However, mosaic patterns were not used until the times of Sassanid Sassanid Empire and Roman Empire and Roman

nfluence.

Roman mosaic found at[Calleva Atrebatum](#) in the [Roman province](#) of [Britannia](#)

Ceramics and ceramic art form which uses small pieces of materials placed together to create a unified whole. The materials commonly used are marble or other stone, glass, [pottery](#), mirror or foil-backed glass, or shells.

The word mosaic[Now ceramics] is from the Italian mosaico deriving from the Latin mosaicus and ultimately from the Greek mouseios meaning belonging to the [Muses](#), hence artistic. The term for each piece of material is [Tessera](#) (plural: tesserae). The term for the spaces in between where the grout goes is the interstices. [Andamento](#) is the word used to describe the movement and flow of [Tesserae](#). The 'opus', the Latin for 'work', is the way in which the pieces are cut and placed.

Common techniques include:

- [Opus regulatum](#): A grid; all tesserae align both vertically and horizontally.
- [Opus tessellatum](#): Tesserae form vertical or horizontal rows, but not both.
- [Opus vermiculatum](#): One or more lines of tesserae follow the edge of a special shape (letters or a major central graphic).
- [Opus musivum](#): Vermiculatum extends throughout the entire background.
- [Opus palladianum](#): Instead of forming rows, tesserae are irregularly shaped. Also known as "crazy paving".
- [Opus sectile](#): A major shape (e.g. heart, letter, cat) is formed by a single tessera, as later in [pietra dura](#).
- [Opus classicum](#): When vermiculatum is combined with tessellatum or regulatum.

- **Opus circumactum: Tesserae are laid in overlapping semicircles or fan shapes.**
- **Micromosaic: using very small tesserae, in Byzantine icons and Italian panels for jewellery from the Renaissance on.**

Three techniques

Tool table for ancient roman mosaics at Roman villa of La Olmeda in Pedrosa de la Vega, Province of Palencia (Castile and León, Spain).

There are three main methods: the direct method, the indirect method and the double indirect method.

Direct method

A 'Direct Method' mosaic courtyard made from irregular pebbles and stone strips, Li Jiang, Yunnan, PRC (China)

The direct method of mosaic construction involves directly placing (gluing) the individual tesserae onto the supporting surface. This method is well suited to surfaces that have a three-dimensional quality, such as vases. This was used for the historic European wall and ceiling mosaics, following underdrawings of the main outlines on the wall below, which are often revealed again when the mosaic falls away.

The direct method suits small projects that are transportable. Another advantage of the direct method is that the resulting mosaic is progressively visible, allowing for any adjustments to tile color or placement.

The disadvantage of the direct method is that the artist must work directly at the chosen surface, which is often not practical for long periods of time, especially for large-scale projects. Also, it is difficult to control the evenness of the finished surface. This is of particular importance when creating a functional surface such as a floor or a table top.

A modern version of the direct method, sometimes called "double direct," is to work directly onto fiberglass mesh. The mosaic can then be constructed with the design visible on the surface and transported to its final location. Large work can be done in this way, with the mosaic being cut up for shipping and then reassembled for installation. It enables the artist to work in comfort in a studio rather than at the site of installation.

Indirect method

The indirect method of applying tesserae is often used for very large projects, projects with repetitive elements or for areas needing site specific shapes. Tiles are applied face-down to a backing paper using an adhesive, and later transferred onto walls, floors or craft projects. This method is most useful for extremely large projects as it gives the maker time to rework areas, allows the cementing of the tiles to the backing panel to be carried out quickly in one operation and helps ensure that the front surfaces of the mosaic tiles and mosaic pieces are flat and in the same plane on the front, even when using tiles and pieces of differing thicknesses. Mosaic murals, benches and tabletops are some of the items usually made using the indirect method, as it results in a smoother and more even surface.

Double indirect method

The double indirect method can be used when it is important to see the work during the creation process as it will appear when completed. The tesserae are placed face-up on a medium (often adhesive-backed paper, sticky plastic or soft lime or putty) as it will appear when installed. When the mosaic is complete, a similar medium is placed atop it. The piece is then turned over, the original underlying material is carefully removed, and the piece is installed as in the indirect method described above. In comparison to the indirect method, this is a complex system to use and requires great skill on the part of the operator, to avoid damaging the work. Its greatest advantage lies in the possibility of the operator directly controlling the final result of the work, which is important e.g. when the human figure is involved.

Mathematics

The best way to arrange variously shaped tiles on a surface can lead to complicated mathematical problems - see tessellation for details. Roger Penrose is a British mathematician who has worked with tiling problems - see Penrose tilings.

The artist M. C. Escher was influenced by Moorish mosaics to begin his investigations into tessellation.

The maze designer and artist Adrian Fisher creates modern mosaic using a system involving three principal shapes (Pyramid, Fin and Mitre).

Digital imaging

A mosaic in digital imaging is a plurality of non-overlapping images, arranged in some tessellation. A photomosaic is a picture made up of various other pictures (pioneered by Joseph Francis), in which each "pixel" is another picture, when examined closely. This form has been adopted in many modern media and digital image searches.

A tile mosaic is a digital image made up of individual tiles, arranged in a non-overlapping fashion, e.g. to make a static image on a shower room or bathing pool floor, by breaking the image down into square pixels formed from ceramic tiles (a typical size is 1 in × 1 in (25 mm × 25 mm), as for example, on the floor of the University of Toronto pool, though sometimes larger tiles such as 2 in × 2 in (51 mm × 51 mm) are used). These digital images are coarse in resolution and often simply express text, such as the depth of the pool in various places, but some such digital images are used to show a sunset or other beach theme.

Recent developments in digital image processing have led to the ability to design physical tile mosaics using computer aided design(CAD) software. The software typically takes as inputs a source bitmap and a palette of colored tiles. The software makes a best-fitmatch of the tiles to the source image.

Robotic manufacturing

With high cost of labor in developed countries, production automation has become increasingly popular. Rather than being assembled by hand, mosaics designed using computer aided design (CAD) software can be assembled by robot. Production can be greater than 10 times faster with higher accuracy. But these "computer" mosaics have a different look than hand-made "artisanal" mosaics. With robotic production, colored tiles are loaded into buffers, and then the robot picks and places tiles individually according to a command file from the design software

The Mughal Empire in India lasted from 1526 until (technically) 1858, although from the late 17th century power flowed away from the emperors to local rulers, and later European powers, above all the British Raj, who were the main power in India by the late 18th century. The period is most notable for luxury arts of the court, and Mughal styles heavily influenced localHindu and later Sikh rulers as well. The Mughal miniature began by importing Persian artists, especially a group brought back by Humayun when in exile in Safavid Persia, but soon local artists, many Hindu, were trained in the style. Realistic portraiture, and images of animals and plants, was developed in Mughal art beyond what the Persians had so far achieved, and the size of miniatures increased, sometimes onto canvas. The Mughal court had access to European prints and other art, and these had increasing influence, shown in the gradual introduction of aspects of Western graphical perspective, and a wider range of poses in the human figure. Some Western images were directly copied or borrowed from. As the courts of local Nawabs developed, distinct provincial styles with stronger influence from traditionalIndian painting developed in both Muslim and Hindu princely courts.

The arts of jewelry and hardstone carving of gemstones, such as jasper, jade, adorned with rubies, diamonds and emeralds are mentioned by the Mughal chronicler Abu'l Fazl, and a range of examples survive; the series of hard stone daggers in the form of horses' heads is particularly impressive.

The Mughals were also fine metallurgists they introduced Damascus steel and refined the locally produced Wootz steel, the Mughals also introduced the "bidri" technique of metalwork in which silver motifs are pressed against a black background. Famous Mughal metallurgists like Ali Kashmiri and Muhammed Salih Thatawi created the seamless celestial globes.

Safavids and Qajars[edit]

Entrance to Sheykh Lotfollah mosque,Naqsh-e Jahan Square, Isfahan

The Iranian Safavids, a dynasty stretching from 1501 to 1786, is distinguished from the Mughal and Ottoman Empires, and earlier Persian rulers, in part through the Shi'a faith of its shahs, which they succeeded in making the majority denomination in Persia. Ceramic arts are marked by the strong influence of Chinese porcelain, often executed in blue and white. Architecture flourished, attaining a high point with the building program of Shah Abbas inIsfahan, which included numerous gardens, palaces (such as Ali Qapu), an immense bazaar, and a large imperial mosque.

The art of manuscript illumination also achieved new heights, in particular in the Shah Tahmasp Shahnameh, an immense copy of Ferdowsi's poem containing more than 250 paintings. In the 17th century a new type of painting develops, based around the album ([muraqqa](#)). The albums were the creations of conoisseurs who bound together single sheets containing paintings, drawings, or calligraphy by various artists, sometimes excised from earlier books, and other times created as independent works. The paintings of [Reza Abbasi](#) figure largely in this new art of the book, depicting one or two larger figures, typically idealized beauties in a garden setting, often using the [grisaille](#) techniques previously used for border paintings for the background.

After the fall of the Safavids, the [Qajars](#), a [Turkmen](#) tribe established from centuries on the banks of the [Caspian Sea](#), assumed power. Qajar art displays an increasing European influence, as in the large oil paintings portraying the Qajar shahs. Steelwork also assumed a new importance. Like the Ottomans, the Qajar dynasty survived until 1925, a few years after the First World War.

Modern period[[edit](#)]

Moroccan [zellige](#) or [girih](#) work

From the 15th century, the number of smaller Islamic courts began to fall, as the Ottoman Empire, and later the Safavids and European powers, swallowed them up; this had an effect on Islamic art, which was usually strongly led by the patronage of the court. From at least the 18th century onwards, elite Islamic art was increasingly influenced by European styles, and in the applied arts either largely adopted Western styles, or ceased to develop, retaining whatever style was prevalent at some point in the late 18th or early 19th centuries. Many industries with very long histories, such as pottery in Iran, largely closed, while others, like metalwork in brass, became generally frozen in style, with much of their production going to tourists or exported as oriental exotica.

The carpet industry has remained large, but mostly uses designs that originated before 1700, and competes with machine-made imitations both locally and around the world. Arts and crafts with a broader social base, like the zellige mosaic tiles of the Maghreb, have often survived better. Islamic countries have developed modern and contemporary art, with very vigorous art worlds in some countries, but the degree to which these should be grouped in a special category as "Islamic art" is questionable, although many artists deal with Islam-related themes, and use traditional elements such as calligraphy. Especially in the oil-rich parts of the Islamic world much modern architecture and interior decoration makes use of motifs and elements drawn from the heritage of Islamic art.

Islamic art encompasses the visual arts produced from the 7th century onwards by people who lived within the territory that was inhabited by or ruled by culturally Islamic populations.[1] It is thus a very difficult art to define because it covers many lands and various peoples over some 1400 years; it is not art specifically of a religion, or of a time, or of a place, or of a single medium like painting. The huge field of Islamic architecture is the subject of a separate article, leaving fields as varied as calligraphy, painting, glass, ceramics, and textiles, among others.

Islamic art is not at all restricted to religious art, but includes all the art of the rich and varied cultures of Islamic societies as well. It frequently includes secular elements and elements that are frowned upon, if not forbidden, by some Islamic theologians. Apart from the ever-present calligraphic inscriptions, specifically religious art is actually less prominent in Islamic art than in Western medieval art, with the exception of Islamic architecture where mosques and their complexes of surrounding buildings are the most common remains. Figurative painting may cover religious scenes, but normally in essentially secular contexts such as the walls of palaces or illuminated books of poetry. The calligraphy and decoration of manuscript Qu'rans is an important aspect, but other religious art such as glass mosque lamps and other mosque fittings such as tiles (e.g. Girih tiles), woodwork and carpets usually have the same style and motifs as contemporary secular art, although with religious inscriptions even more prominent.

There are repeating elements in Islamic art, such as the use of geometrical floral or vegetal designs in a repetition known as the arabesque. The arabesque in Islamic art is often used to symbolize the transcendent, indivisible and infinite nature of God.[9] Mistakes in repetitions may be intentionally introduced as a show of humility by artists who believe only God can produce perfection, although this theory is disputed.

The earliest grand Islamic buildings, like the Dome of the Rock, in Jerusalem had interior walls decorated with mosaics in the

Byzantine style, but without human figures. From the 9th century onwards the distinctive Islamic tradition of glazed and brightly coloured tiling for interior and exterior walls and domes developed. Some earlier schemes create designs using mixtures of tiles each of a single colour that are either cut to shape or are small and of a few shapes, used to create abstract geometric patterns. Later large painted schemes use tiles painted before firing with a part of the scheme – a technique requiring confidence in the consistent results of firing.

Some elements, especially the letters of inscriptions, may be moulded in three dimensionalrelief, and in especially in Persia certain tiles in a design may have figurative painting of animals or single human figures. These were often part of designs mostly made up of tiles in plain colours but with larger fully painted tiles at intervals. The larger tiles are often shaped as eight-pointed stars, and may show animals or a human head or bust, or plant or other motifs. The geometric patterns, such as modern North African zellige work, made of small tiles each of a single colour but different and regular shapes, are often referred to as "mosaic", which is not strictly correct.

The Indian subcontinent, some northern parts of which conquered by the Ghaznavids and Ghurids in the 9th century, did not become autonomous until 1206, when the Muizzi, or slave-kings, seized power, marking the birth of the Delhi Sultanate. Later other competing sultanates were founded in Bengal, Kashmir, Gujarat, Jaunpur, Malwa, and in the north Deccan (the Bahmanids). They separated themselves little by little from Persian traditions, giving birth to an original approach to architecture and urbanism, marked in particular by interaction with Hindu art. Study of the production of objects has hardly begun, but a lively art of manuscript illumination is known. The period of the sultanates ended with the arrival of the Mughals, who progressively seized their territories.

16th century Turkish Iznik tiles, which would have originally formed part of a much larger group.

CERAMICS IN BANGLADESH [PRESENT POSITION]BY [Zakir Hossain Bhuiyan]

Ceramic Industry manufacture of useful and ornamental articles from clay by shaping and hardening it in high temperature. The industry is basically a development of indigenous pottery works. Broadly, ceramics denote the manufacture of any product made from a non-metallic mineral hardened at high temperatures. Industrial ceramics comprise all industrially used solid materials that are neither metallic nor organic. Major ceramic products include glass, earthenware, porcelain, and white-ware, porcelain enamels, brick tiles and terracotta, refractories, cement, lime and gypsum.

The art of POTTERY is perhaps as old as human civilisation. Initially, it started with clay and then passed through stages of moulding various media like WOOD, stone, shell and metal before reaching the age of ceramic and porcelain. Bengal passed through all these stages before reaching the ceramic age. Ceramic industry took a formal start in this country in 1958 with the establishment of Tajma Ceramic Industries Ltd. at BOGRA. It is the oldest modern ceramic manufacturing plant in Bangladesh and is also the only ceramic factory located in North Bengal. Its production was very small and the quality of the product was not good. The Pakistan Ceramic Industries Ltd. was established in early 1960s and it went into production in 1966. It manufactured ceramic products for the domestic market. It was renamed as Peoples Ceramic Industries Ltd after the independence of Bangladesh.

In 2011, Bangladesh has 21 ceramic industry units. Six of them are fairly large and these are Monno Ceramic Industries, Shinepukur Ceramic Industries, Bengal Fine Ceramic Industries, Standard Ceramic Industries, Far Ceramic Industries and Peoples Ceramic Industries. These companies produce high quality ceramic and porcelain wares. The annual production is about 15,000 tons of ceramic items. About 5,000 tons is exported to 45 countries. The remaining amount is consumed locally. Initially, all ceramic industries catered to the domestic market only.

The Tajma Ceramic Industries has a showroom and an export department in DHAKA. It has been manufacturing porcelain tableware since 1958. Although it is the oldest producer of ceramics, the factory manufactures only about 12,000 pieces (4 m tons) of assorted tableware per day, which is about half the capacity of other major ceramic tableware manufacturing plants. The company has been catering mainly to the domestic market. The Peoples Ceramic Industries, located in Tongi Industrial Area, about 20 km north of Dhaka, is one of the oldest and largest ceramic companies in Bangladesh. The factory went into production in 1986. The production capacity of the factory is about 28,000 pieces of assorted tableware per day. The company however, has had little success in the export markets. Recently, the company has developed a new brand 'Super China', which is drawing the attention of foreign buyers. Bengal Fine Ceramics Ltd. is the first industry in the country to make soft porcelain, which the company calls 'stoneware'. This is an off-white product manufactured by using local Mymensingh clay. The factory went into production in 1986. It produces about 24,000 pieces (6 m tons) of stoneware per day. From the very beginning, the company concentrated its trading activities in the international market and has been quite successful in its endeavour. Recently, the company has established a sister concern, Standard Ceramic Industries Ltd., near GAZIPUR, about 30 km north of Dhaka.

The largest and most successful ceramic company in Bangladesh is the Monno Ceramic Industries Ltd, which started production in 1985 and manufactures very high quality porcelain tableware. This company has done well in the export market with its sales office in London and a permanent stall in the Frankfurt House-wares show. Shinepukur Ceramics Ltd was incorporated in 1997 with the aim of establishing a world-class bone china and porcelain tableware industry.

The company is located at Beximco Industrial Park, Gazipur. It started its porcelain and bone china units in April 1999 and November 1999 respectively. Since the beginning of its commercial operations in 1999, the company has distinguished itself as the fastest growing concern in the sector. It has captured about 60% of the domestic market share and is doing well in the global ceramic tableware markets.

About 95% of raw materials for making quality and exportable ceramic products in Bangladesh are imported from abroad. The materials are imported mainly from Japan, Germany, New Zealand, South Korea and India. The prime raw materials of ceramic products are white clay and sand. The largest deposit of white clay in Bangladesh was first discovered in 1957 at Bijoypur of MYMENSINGH. The total reserve of white clay from this region is estimated to be 2.57 million tons. Clay was also found in jaflong of SYLHET. But there is no clay or sand treatment plant at these places.

To ensure proper quality and goodwill all ceramic tableware producing units use high quality raw materials. The machinery and equipment are also modern and conform to the latest technology and standard. Each of the units has its own in-house laboratory facility, quality control and testing mechanism. The products that are being marketed now are: dinner sets, tea sets, coffee sets, soup sets, fruit sets, plates, bowls, flower vases, mugs and various types of souvenir items. Most ceramic products are ovenproof, chill-proof and dishwasher-proof and free from any chemical hazards.

At present, Bangladesh is exporting ceramic tableware to more than 45 countries, including the USA, Italy, Spain, France, New Zealand, the Netherlands, Australia and Sweden.

MODERN CERAMICE USED IN BENGAL

www.ingramcontent.com/pod-product-compliance
Lightning Source LLC
Chambersburg PA
CBHW060821290526
45792CB00005BB/1743